Putting health at the heart of your practice
Sheila Scott

Putting health at the heart of your practice

Published by Dental Protection Limited
© Dental Protection 2014
All rights reserved

Sheila Scott asserts her moral right to be identified as the author of this book

Except for the quotation of short passages for the purposes of criticism and review, no part of this manuscript may be reproduced in any form by any electronic and mechanical means (including photocopying, recording, or information storage and retrieval) without the permission in writing from the publisher or the author

ISBN 978-0-9929321-0-7

Designed by Daniel Welton of
www.eightdesign.com
Set in 10.5 on 12pt, Helvetica 55

Printed and bound in Great Britain by Printwells Limited

The opinions expressed in this work are the opinion of the author and may not necessarily reflect the views of Dental Protection. The author is not a dentist and her views on dentistry are expressed from a patient's viewpoint which may not be quite as informed as those of a qualified professional

Sheila Scott

Sheila has spent the last two decades helping hundreds of dental practices to 'up' their game. Her consultancy is based on the conviction, backed up by her own research that the key to success lies in building an appreciative and loyal patient base.

In one neat tome, which serves as an introduction for the uninitiated and a revision course for the converted, she explains how a dental practice can be successful.

A psychology graduate with a postgraduate diploma in marketing, Sheila wrote her first book 'Where to Next?' in the 1980s to help hundreds of young dentists take their first steps out of Dental School and into hospital and practice careers.

Moving into consultancy in 1989, Sheila started asking patients what they really wanted from dental practices... and the results have never stopped surprising her audiences. Her consultancy and this book are all based on what patients want, not what dental teams think they want.

Sheila lives in her native north of Scotland, travelling every week throughout the UK and abroad to visit practices and deliver lectures, workshops and seminars.

See www.sheila-scott.co.uk for more details.

Dental Protection Limited

Dental Protection Limited is part of the world's leading professional indemnity organisation for doctors, dentists, dental hygienists, dental therapists and other healthcare professionals.

Over 70% of the UK dental team use Dental Protection. We also serve members in 70 countries world-wide.

As the international leader in dental risk management, Dental Protection has created a large portfolio of risk management and educational resources to help the dental team meet the needs for further development.

At Dental Protection we believe risk management is an important part of running a safer more successful practice.

Visit our website and get to know us even better
www.dentalprotection.org

DPL Xtra

DPL Xtra is a practice programme that rewards dental practices who adopt a proactive approach to risk management.

By creating a safer environment for patients, the dental team is exposed to less risk. We reward this commitment by reducing the subscriptions payable by dentists, hygienists, therapists, orthodontic therapists, clinical dental technicians and registered dental nurses working in the practice.

Access to free indemnity is also available for employed, non-registered staff including practice managers, trainee dental nurses and receptionists working in a practice with DPL Xtra membership.

There are many other benefits such as online support for practice managers, and access to free online CPD.

Discover how your practice can benefit from DPL Xtra
www.dentalprotection.org/uk/dplxtra

Foreword by Kevin Lewis

Sheila Scott and I have been travelling on parallel but (as I am now rapidly starting to appreciate) gradually converging courses during our respective professional lives. I graduated with a degree in dentistry, Sheila with a degree in psychology.

My undergraduate life had been spent in the dental school (The London Hospital, later to become The Royal London Hospital and latterly St Barts and The Royal London) which was at that time the epicentre of preventive dentistry in the UK.

It was little wonder after spending four or five years in that intoxicating environment that I emerged with a burning passion to create a practice with whole-family preventive dental care at its heart. It opened its doors just under three years after I qualified, and I remained there for about 18 years.

Like Sheila, I spent many years on a mission to inspire other like-minded colleagues to embrace preventive dentistry and place it at the heart of their clinical practice.

During those 18 years, and a similar number of years after that, I developed another passion – this time for dental practice management and introducing the principles of good business management and key insights from the business world outside dentistry, into the task of running a dental practice.

I have been extremely fortunate to have had ample opportunities over the past 30 years or so, to communicate these ideas to and with my dental colleagues, through my own writing and lecturing.

It was in this arena that I became aware of Sheila and her work with dental practices, and how highly regarded she was by those who had worked with her.

Her mastery of the psychology of marketing and practice promotion, underpinned by a strong belief that we should treat others as we would wish to be treated ourselves, have proved to be a powerful and effective combination.

Our paths still cross, perhaps too occasionally given our geographical separation, but I am in no doubt that we are kindred spirits.

The second half of my own career to date has been spent in the dento-legal field, firstly serving on the Board of Dental Protection Limited, but then becoming a dento-legal adviser and (since 1998) the Dental Director. This has been a wonderful journey of yet more discovery and it was not long before I came to realise that the things that help to create a really successful dental practice – all the things that I had been talking about in connection with dental practice management – are also the very things that help dentists to keep their patients happy and satisfied, thereby keeping their dento-legal risks to a minimum too.

I wholeheartedly endorse Sheila's mantra that '*It's not about the dentistry*'. In her own insightful and compelling fashion she has put her finger on one of the most important (if counter-intuitive) truths for anyone who aspires to be a successful dentist or to own and operate a successful and profitable dental practice.

Foreword by Kevin Lewis

The central messages of this short book are as powerful as they are simple and easy to grasp, and anyone who takes them to heart and mind is on course for a successful career in dental practice, treating appreciative patients who place a real value on the care they receive and taking responsibility for their own oral health in the spirit of partnership.

Selling them something they want (health) rather than something they don't want (dentistry) makes sense.

We at Dental Protection did not take lightly the decision to facilitate the publication of this book, but I am confident that many people will stand to benefit from that unusual decision.

Most obviously, the dentists who take the time to read, think about and act upon its contents, but also all those other members of their practice teams. Collectively their change of focus will benefit more patients than we will ever know.

Dentists who place patients, their wellbeing and their oral health at the heart of their practice, will have much less need for the services of organisations such as Dental Protection.

Dentistry is certainly more about people than teeth, and yet so many dentists continue to ignore this fact and pursue self-centred goals instead. They do so at their peril.

There is no shortage of evidence that building rapport and strong relationships with patients is the key to success whichever way you care to view it. When this is based on trust and mutual respect and the shared goal of optimising the patient's oral health, the seeds of enduring success are sown and the potential for complaints and litigation can be dramatically reduced.

Kevin Lewis
BDS LDSRCS FDSRCS(Eng) FFGDP(UK)

This book is dedicated to

> Caroline Holland, who provided the idea, the stimulation and the continual encouragement, advice and reviews for this book. Without her professionalism and friendship, the draft would still be half finished and full of typos, languishing on a laptop computer twice taken on holiday.
> www.carolineholland.eu

and

> Gordon Nicol, who took me and the laptop computer on holidays and was eventually persuaded that I wouldn't be bored while he went diving. Thanks, Gorgeous!

Contents

Introduction
12 It's not about the dentistry

Chapter one
15 The case for the health focus

Chapter two
20 From check-up to dental health check (DHC)

Chapter three
25 The dental health check – the opening conversation

Chapter four
37 The physical checks

Chapter five
42 Making the DHC your own

Chapter six
46 Making the DHC happen

Chapter seven
53 Building hygiene

Chapter eight
58 The hygiene protocol

Chapter nine
65 Dental plans

Chapter ten
69 One more thing – sterilisation and patient protection

Chapter eleven
74 Conclusion

I have worked in the dental field for 25 years and, in that time, built a detailed understanding of what makes a successful dental practice.

At the outset, I mostly worked with principals who wanted to convert to private care.

More recently, I have helped all kinds of practices through a myriad of challenges including improving profits, addressing staffing issues or partnership challenges.

Although my first degree was in psychology, I trained as a marketer and, wherever I go, essential marketing principles are also applied to the advice I provide. That means focusing the majority of my attention on the customer – or in dentistry, the patient.

It means focusing on what patients think about their own dentist, and what they want from their dentist and the practice. In the light of the General Dental Council's standards, published 30 September 2013, seeing the dental experience from the patient's point of view has never been so critical.

When I began compiling this book around my consultancy, my working title was 'It's not about the dentistry'. The title has evolved to 'Putting health at the heart of your practice' in order to sum up what, above all else, I stand for.

Although my working title has changed, I would still like to stress that what you do really isn't about the dentistry.

The point is that patients, the source of your livelihood, don't judge you on your clinical ability – they don't have this knowledge to assess you; they judge you on everything else. How do you respond to this?

How do you convey you care for them so well that their wellbeing is your priority?

This book was written to answer those questions, and more.

Sheila Scott
Business consultant

It is ironic that in this day of high-tech, complex, and costly dental procedures and treatments, simple, inexpensive, easily-understood actions, such as effective oral hygiene and quitting smoking, could have such a huge impact on the quality of life and the cost of dental health care.
David Croser

You only get the patients you deserve.
Sheila Scott

Chapter one
The case for the health focus

The case for the health focus

Do you ever think you know too much about dentistry? Strange question, you may think, because no one can ever know too much about his or her chosen profession. But, when a dental practice has lost its way and needs some redirection, my top-line diagnosis is often that they know too much. By this, I mean that dentists can be so immersed in delivering treatment, they overlook what matters to the patient. In fact, as well as this oversight, they also don't really know what matters, although they think they do. This conclusion is based on my own research. For the past 25 years, I have been conducting patient questionnaires to find out what really matters to patients, and what patients think.

<u>The top eight things that patients tell me are very important to them</u>
(percentages of patients rating the aspect very important).

1 Trusting the dentist 92%
2 Ensuring healthy teeth and gums 82%
3 General cleanliness and hygiene 80%
4 Treatments to solve dental problems 79%
5 Being seen quickly in an emergency 78%
6 Sterilisation and patient protection 74%
7 Special skills of dentist 71%
8 Screening for oral cancer 63%

Data taken from Sheila Scott's research 2008–2011. 2010–2011 average figures shown above.

When working with practices, I produce a jumbled list of these – and other qualities – and ask the dental teams to rank them as their patients would. In far too many cases, teams are wide of the mark. In fact, if I reversed their lists, they would often be more accurate. Worryingly, team members and dentists often fail to agree. This suggests to me that, when working side-by-side, delivering care to patients, they are undermining each other. What a waste of energy! What potential for misunderstanding in the team as well as with patients.

Patients tell me they want two things more than any other. Firstly, they want to trust their dentist and the dental practice team. Secondly, they want care and treatments to ensure their teeth and gums stay healthy. This comes as a surprise to most dental professionals, who invariably believe patients are more interested in cosmetic or restorative dentistry. When patients walk into a dental practice, what they are hoping for is a *clean bill of health*. They are thinking: *I hope the dentist doesn't find anything*. The health professional has the opportunity to deliver care (and treatment, when necessary) in a way that proves to the patient, beyond any doubt, that the clean bill of health is what both parties are hoping for. But, too often, they fail to exploit this opportunity. This is because dental teams have their own agenda for patient care, usually a heavy focus on the provision of treatment and increasingly, cosmetic treatment. Treatment has come to dominate the ethos and marketing strategies of practices in recent decades. Dentists seem to me to be consummate problem solvers. In dental school they are taught to seek problems to fix, and most approach the opportunity with relish – a chance to demonstrate their technical expertise.

For almost all dentists, the high point is a dental problem that will need their professional skill and expertise and the best technical designs, materials or lab work to produce a clinically perfect reconstruction. Some dentists can hardly contain their delight when they spot a problem to be fixed – and many celebrate the finished filling, crown, denture, inlay, onlay, root treatment or other solution with a flourish – like a magician pulling a rabbit out of a particularly difficult hat. *Voila!* says their body language; be impressed!

While the dentist has satisfied their desire to provide care and treatment, the patient, far from experiencing admiration, is more likely to think: That was a bit of an ordeal or *Why is my body failing?* or *When will my mouth feel normal again?* or *That wasn't something I really wanted to have to pay for* or even *This person was obviously just looking for things to fix in my mouth, so that he/she can make money out of me*. Previous NHS regulations and traditional private pricing systems promote treatment so there is almost a pre-programming in the brains of dentists to respond positively to opportunities for treatment – they continually seek problems to fix. Another barrier to embracing the health focus in practice would appear to be the apparent failure, so far, of good hygiene advisory messages. 'Why,' asks the dentist, '*if patients are so interested in health, do they not brush their darned teeth?*' My response to this is that the failure to understand how to maintain dental health does not lie with the patient, but with dental professionals who have systematically failed to get their messages across to patients.

Action points
Make sure you know what matters to patients – and that everyone in the team is 'on the same page'

Find ways to communicate that you care about your patients' dental health – for more ideas, read on

Every dentist and therapist/hygienist can remember at least one patient who suddenly 'gets the message' about looking after their own mouth, and who turns into a model patient ¬thereafter. If only this could be achieved systematically, dentists would be providing exactly what patients are looking for, and both patient and dentist would benefit.

I'm not a dentist. I've never been trained in dentistry. All my views on dental care have been gained from conversations with practising dentists; from listening to dental lectures and from listening to patients.

I've worked with very preventively focused practices whose teams discuss health with patients, tell patients they are trying to prevent the need for treatment, encourage all patients to keep regular hygiene visits and show them how to remove dental and interdental plaque daily to achieve good oral health. I've also worked with cosmetically focused practices whose teams pay as much attention to helping keep their patients healthy for the long term as they do in providing a 'makeover'. Both these types of practices are very successful. But, in my experience, most general dental practices could do more to prove to patients they are primarily concerned with keeping patients healthy. Most general practices have become too engrossed in chasing the path to restorative perfection or aesthetic profit. They chase the 'problems' that patients may or may not perceive they have. They overlook what matters most to patients. It's time to reclaim the focus on health.

Chapter two
From check-up to dental health check

To start developing the focus on health, I suggest the concept of the 'routine' appointment or 'check-up' is banished. Most practices quite rightly pay a great deal of attention to the new patient appointment, through introducing treatment co-ordination or using practice meetings to find ways to improve the new patient experience. However, most practices fail to develop a similarly impressive journey for their existing patients or for their new patients' subsequent appointments, leaving them at risk of failing to return (regularly) or seeing them leave for a new, more impressive, practice. The regular exam appointment has to be the most important appointment to get right for patients. It is the one that patients keep most frequently and, therefore, the one at which, I believe, dentists' reputations are made or broken. I often remind dentists, who have been in practice for 20 years or more, that if their longstanding patients have stayed with them for all that time, they will have experienced up to 40 exams but, hopefully, only five or six incidences of treatment. This is why the exam appointment is key and why it is essential the patient feels the dentist is just as interested in seeing them as they are at fixing things or doing treatment. Sadly, I find too many dentists are bored by exam appointments. They know these are not exciting treatment appointments (yet, without exams, what treatment need can be determined?) and believe these appointments do not tax their best skills (but isn't accurate assessment and diagnosis the most taxing intellectual skill of all?). Again, perhaps as a result of accepting low fees for exams to date, most dentists try to do these appointments as quickly as possible, keeping costs to patients low. In my opinion, speedy exams mean less feedback and information to patients.

From check-up to dental health check

Less feedback and information to patients may mean a cheap service – but also an unimpressive one. As in all instances where information or communication is bypassed, the patients will draw their own conclusions. Unfortunately, the immediate conclusion may be that the dentist isn't interested in them or doesn't have time for them. I have been developing a new regular exam experience with practices for the past 15 years or so – creating a framework that introduces feedback on the experience. I felt it was very important to change the language of the 'check-up', which I remember from when I was a little girl in the north of Scotland during the 1960s. In those days, check-ups routinely took 30 seconds or less (or so it seemed) to complete – and consisted of an apparently quick poke around the mouth and a look for holes to fill. In fact, I was 23 (in 1983) before I met a dentist who told me there were other aspects to check-ups, and talked to me about dental health and prevention. Shortly after this, I started working with dentists and discovered there was more to dentistry than holes and fillings. Yet, even in this second decade of the 21st century, when we ask patients what their dentist was looking at or checking during their last appointment, the routine response from patients is:

1 Teeth
2 Gums
3 Oral cancer (only rarely)

And, when we ask patients what they feel the purpose of the exam or check-up is, their response is invariably 'looking for holes' or 'fillings' or 'to find work that needs doing'. First of all, the key three perceived assessments are only a part of what dentists are actually doing during an exam. This means there's a huge opportunity to help patients be more appreciative of this appointment. Secondly, note how the one thing the patients believe dentists are looking for (holes) reflects my view of dentistry in the 1960s. If patients believe dentists' priority is to identify holes – problems, in other words – what incentive is there for patients to return for regular exams or screening for which they will have to pay/take time off work? No wonder dentists are finding it difficult to keep patients on their recommended recall schedule and committed to regular hygiene visits!

The naming of the first key appointment
In the mid-1990s, I began searching for an alternative word to replace 'check-up' and 'examination', both of which I felt had negative connotations for patients. Eventually, and together with the practices that helped pioneer this approach, I decided the words 'dental health' should always be the prefix to whatever other word the practice liked to use, whether Dental Health Check, Dental Health Appointment or Dental Health Exam. 'Dental' must be included because this was how the patients thought of the experience. I know the more clinically correct word would be oral, but then that is understood less well by patients than dental – and it can also lead to other thoughts and definitions that are definitely not useful to the dental experience! 'Health' is an essential part of the appointment and reinforces the positive aspect of the visit to both patients and practitioners.

From check-up to dental health check

Action points

Cultivate appreciation among patients for the care you provide by making sure they know you are checking for the health of many aspects of the mouth – as opposed to looking for problems to fix

Consider abolishing the words exam or check-up and replacing with Dental Health Check (DHC) or another name that indicates you are taking a holistic approach – read on

Finally, after testing many different final words to describe the experience, I began to realise that receptionists were finding some of the more ambitious words difficult to use with patients, who inevitably came into the practice talking about their 'check-ups'. We finally settled on Dental Health Check as the preferred name for the appointment so receptionists, in particular, could say the words without seeming to contradict the patient who might come in for the next 10 years for a 'check-up'. Shortened to a snappy 'DHC', it now sounded bigger and broader than check-up – that was, after all, our aim.

Chapter three
The dental health check
– the opening conversation

The dental health check – the opening conversation

How do you usually open the conversation with your patients in the surgery? I mean, after the essential social rapport-building and relaxing chit-chat of 'Hello, Mrs Patient, how are you doing today? Come on in and take a seat...' etc.
Do you start with the universal opening line, and indication of the purpose of the visit: 'Any problems?' I don't think this is a useful way to introduce the appointment. This may helpfully signal the start of the real business of the appointment, but it also confirms to patients that the dentist really is looking for work. It has been interesting to observe increasing numbers of dentists trying to soften this question, as if they are aware they may be too blunt. So, they ask: 'Any concerns or sensitivities?' I admit I also hate 'Anything to report?', 'What can I do for you today?' or 'Anything to tell me?' as I believe the professional has a duty of care and should be specific. It is not satisfactory to leave the patient to decide what is or isn't important. Why should patients, have to do all the work in identifying key areas to bring up and discuss? My recommendation, as a preliminary opening line, is to always make the first question of the appointment a very pointed one about health.

1 **'How healthy do you feel your teeth and gums are?'**
This reinforces what the appointment should be all about, helping the patient to maintain a healthy mouth for life. It also forces some patients to take personal responsibility for their dental health, starting with a self-assessment. The ideal patient will respond with: 'Ooh, I think I'm okay, but I have a little bit of bleeding up here.'

And they will definitely understand the real focus of the appointment and whole dental service. The recalcitrant patient who complains that 'You're the dentist, and you should be able to tell' may need some further persuasion, and I would suggest that dentists respond with: 'I'll tell you what I think, and I'll also show you how you can tell, too. Is that okay?' Following successful use of this first question about health, a framework can be developed for a full Dental Health Check covering all aspects of dental health. My suggestions are detailed below, although practices should always work out their own protocols based on what is in the head, the heart and the hands of the clinicians in the practice.

2 'Any problems?'
This question now makes sense as it follows a general discussion about health. As the dental professional, you need to know if there are any symptoms of disease or dysfunction. Looking for problems to fix is now seen as secondary to the desire to check their health.

3 Medical status update
All practices routinely check medical details, whether by questionnaire/updated questionnaires or verbal questions. When it is the job of team members to ask patients for updated medical information, practices should have a sentence or two of explanation at hand to let patients know why these updates are important. Please, do not continually tell patients that the information is needed because it's a legal requirement (box ticking) or that it is needed to prevent the practice killing the patient ('In case something happens to you whilst you're here', or '(There may be some things we can't do to you if it interacts with your meds').

The dental health check – the opening conversation

3 Instead, my practices are positive and honest with a health-based rationale. They tell patients: 'There are lots of medical conditions and medications you might be taking that do affect dental health and, if we are to do a complete assessment of your dental health each time, we need to know about these.' I dislike the use of the standard term 'medical history' during dental appointments. When patients hear the word 'history', they immediately start thinking of a long time ago – and will, therefore, start to tell you about their real history. Whilst this may be useful once, what dentists really need, on a regular basis, is up-to-date information on what has changed medically since the patient's last visit. The defence organisations will advise that the full list of medical conditions and drug areas should be checked specifically each time the patient visits the practice, and that patients should sign a full medical update form regularly. I would never contradict their advice, but I believe that four quite specific updating questions will secure the accurate and full information that health professionals need each time, and the use of very specific language will direct the patients' thoughts to produce the necessary information.

These questions are:
1 Can you confirm which pills, potions, lotions or sprays you use or take regularly?
2 Have you seen your doctor or been to a hospital since we last saw you?
3 Could you be pregnant or menopausal? (For women only, obviously)
4 Could you be allergic to anything dentally related such as mouthwash or latex?

The first two of these questions are very different to the standard 'Are you fit and well?' and 'Are you taking any medications?' questions that I hear dentists ask. And they produce very different, and much more useful, answers than the bland general questions. No patients like to think of themselves as anything but fit and well, and generally they do feel fit and well when they visit – most of us just forget about the 15 pills we take every day to stay that way!

So, if you ask us if we're healthy, we're going to say 'Yes' as an immediate response. And if you ask us if we're taking medications we'll say 'No'. You see I believe we are psychologically programmed to protect ourselves from negative self-images and judgements, and from believing we are vulnerable. Dentists have to be specific in the way they ask patients the questions about these areas – they have to help patients supply the answers they need! Dentists usually have a high awareness of the complications – or even danger – inherent in some medications – the risk of necrosis caused by bisphosphonates, for example – and take great care about how and when these complications are discussed with patients. But, they are less likely to discuss the impact on dental health of certain health conditions such as diabetes or heart problems or taking any one of a long list of medications. However, because it could be important to dental health, I encourage all my clients to make sure they regularly draw attention to how much more important it may be to these patients to have their dental health assessed, monitored and managed.

The dental health check – the opening conversation

One of my clients has decided to implement a double 'medical alert' system on her records. As is traditional on records, she uses the red star/red alert field to highlight patients who are medically compromised, but she is also using a green 'health alert' sticker/field for patients who have medical conditions or make lifestyle choices (see below) that may mean the management of periodontal status is particularly important. The green health alert sticker/field prompts and reminds clinicians about discussions regarding gum health and control of plaque and gum inflammation.

It does not matter whether it's the medical questionnaire or verbal questioning that is used for screening; the green sticker/field is a constant reminder that there may be a discussion about the links between dental and medical health. This means the end result is that practice attention and patient awareness of dental health are increased.

4 <u>Lifestyle factors</u>

At the start of this century, it seemed more and more studies, reports and articles were being published on the systemic links and implications of dental health. Therapist/hygienists, in particular, began discussing links between mouth health and heart health with patients, and patients were responding with a great deal of interest. Questions about smoking and alcohol started to appear on medical questionnaires and, increasingly, practices would pitch in to support patients who wanted to quit smoking. Personally, I am not sure if smoking cessation services belong to dentistry (at least, not yet). I think if smokers do wish to give up, they are more likely to turn to their GMP or pharmacist for help, and I think there are bigger battles to be fought in the dental arena.

NB
At the time of writing, some parts of this section are a little controversial in Europe at least, so please, if this tickles your fancy, do your own research into these areas, and make your own clinical decisions as to how you wish to include the latest research on systemic links

But what I do think dentists have a moral and professional duty to do is inform patients of the dental implications of smoking, e.g.: 'Because you smoke, Mr Melley, it's even more important for us to keep an eye on your gum health' or 'Because you smoke and, particularly if you smoke and drink alcohol at the same time, it's even more important you keep up regular dental health visits, so we can keep an eye on your mouth.' Follow this with an explanation of how smoking affects the gums, how gum inflammation is linked with heart health, how and why oral cancer is on the increase and inform them of the importance of keeping regular visits to a dental health professional. Ever increasingly, scientific research from around the world is linking dental health to a plethora of medical conditions and lifestyle factors such as poor nutrition and major stress events. It has also long been understood that gum disease can be inherited or passed from individual to individual within a household. Currently, I am led to believe that some of the evidence is scanty or mixed and that cause and effect is still not fully understood, but no one denies that there are links between gum inflammation and body health, and between gum inflammation and a host of lifestyle choices. So, is it not incumbent upon the health-focused practitioner to mention this emerging thinking to patients? To address this point, some of my practices have decided to screen patients for a number of these lifestyle factors as well as for the associated medical factors. They will ask open-ended questions or make a record of patients who smoke or carry too much weight, are planning a family, are menopausal, have had a recent major stress event, etc, in order to prompt a little gentle discussion about how it may be more important than ever to maintain excellent gum health and reduce any inflammation in the gums. Patients are responding very positively to these discussions.

The dental health check – the opening conversation

It is important to ensure the whole team knows how to discuss these aspects with patients. There is a world of difference between 'If you don't floss, you'll die' and 'If you're stressed, there is a chance that you may be more susceptible to the factors that cause gum problems, and there may also be other health problems linked with it.' Expand upon this with: 'We're beginning to understand that there are links between how the body responds to stress and the potential for heart problems – and they might be similar to how the body responds to gum inflammation. We now believe that, as dental health professionals, we can possibly reduce your risks by helping you control your gum inflammation.' However, this is an emerging and changing field, so it would also be useful to have some literature for patients. Practices can write their own factsheets or start collecting published articles as they appear in the professional or consumer press. The British Dental Health Foundation's website www.dentalhealth.org currently has a useful Healthy *Mouth Healthy Body* leaflet/website section, and www.perio.org has a great collection of literature and some good advice for consumers. I am keenly waiting for advice to the profession regarding discussions with young patients on the topic of HPV, lifestyle choices and oral cancer. However, I am very glad to see this already openly tackled in promotional materials available from www.mouthcancer.org

5 <u>A progress check</u>
We all love to feel cared for and, as dental professionals, we can offer this to patients by actively monitoring progress each time they visit. Just as gyms and weight control classes regularly find out how clients have changed/improved, monitoring progress helps bond patients to their dentist and practice. If you usually turn to your dental nurse to ask if there are any 'watches' recorded on the notes or ask for a status report since the last DHC, make sure you explain to the patient why you're doing this. Formalise this part of the Dental Health Check and tell patients this is what is done every time. It's also an opportunity to praise the patient for maintaining their health.

6 <u>Patient's satisfaction with appearance</u>
Although I believe practices need to focus on health, I also think an aesthetic check should be a part of each and every Dental Health Check, and a non-threatening question should be asked every time. Dentists should offer patients the opportunity to share their thoughts on aesthetics. That said, I disapprove of written or blatant 'Smile Checks' for general patients that ask 10 questions about the aesthetics of teeth without balancing questions about gum health and home care habits. Please keep the very detailed 'Smile Check' for the patient who has expressed an interest in aesthetics, and preferably do this verbally. I often tell the true story of seeing my friend Mandy for lunch (see panel overpage) as it illustrates how easy it is to miss opportunities.

The dental health check – the opening conversation

I hadn't seen Mandy for quite some time, and I thought she looked great. The conversation went as follows... 'Have you lost weight? Changed your hair? What is it?' I asked. 'Had my teeth whitened,' she grinned. 'Wow! What a difference! Maybe I should have it done too?'

This was conversation number one.

Later that evening, I spoke with the Gorgeous One: conversation two.

'I saw Mandy today. She looked great. She's had her teeth whitened. Do you think I should have it done too?'

Four months later I saw my dentist. (Now once in around 1995, he asked me if I wanted to do something about the gap between my front teeth, or the small 2s I have. 'Not interested,' I replied then. So my dentist made a note on my records that the question had been asked, and that I'd responded in the negative. He never asked me again.)

5 *I didn't ask about whitening, because all I was concerned about during my Dental Health Check was whether I'd get away with a clean bill of health and not have a ticking-off for failing to keep plaque under control since my last visit.*

But when I got home, the Gorgeous One remembered: conversation three.

'Are you getting your teeth whitened then?' he asked. 'Oops. I forgot to ask. But then, he didn't ask either – maybe he doesn't do it?'

But the point is, the following week I might walk past the new shop front practice in the local town which has a poster in the window advertising tooth whitening. What do you think I might do?

NB
Some practices may complete more non-clinical checks – each practice must define their own version of the routine Dental Health Check – and some may add further questions or screens such as a homecare habits or routine diet check

I accept that dentists do not necessarily know when their patients have had that lunchtime conversation with the 'Mandy' they know, nor do they know when patients are dating and want to look their best, or when a patients may come into a little money, receive an invitation to a family event or school reunion. In other words, they are totally unaware when a patient's improvable minor imperfections take on a whole new importance. They are also in the dark when the latest *Ten Years Younger*-type television programme finally makes a patient look in the mirror and consider doing something that would have been unacceptable to them 10 years ago.

Raising the topic of cosmetic treatment must not be a hard sell or an attack on a fragile ego. Without permission from the patient, it is not acceptable to point out the patient's aesthetic imperfections, but it is useful to ask patients if appearance is something they wish to discuss.

So, I would suggest asking one of these questions at each Dental Health Check: 'Are you happy with the appearance of your teeth and gums?' or even 'Are you still happy...?' or 'I take it you're still happy...' When this question is one of many, added to a pro forma check list, it becomes routine; the patient sees it as routine and will not react negatively. If, however, a patient does object, you should have an explanation ready such as: 'Mr Greystones, please don't worry. My interest is totally in how fit and healthy your mouth is, but some patients do wish to discuss cosmetic treatments, and I need to prompt a discussion so we can talk about both health and appearance.'

Note how the appearance question can therefore be a trigger to reassure patients yet again that the focus of the practice is on health first.

The dental health check – the opening conversation

Action points
Review the language you use at the start of the appointment and make sure patients know you are interested in their dental health and the factors in their life that may affect this

Make sure you give your patients the opportunity to raise any aesthetic concerns

The only note of caution I would issue regarding the appearance question is that it *must* be used well into the body of the Dental Health Check. If used too soon, or as an opening question, the patient may feel the pressure of the sell, whereas you only want him or her to know you are happy to discuss their mouth from every aspect.

So, the dentist has yet to look inside the patient's mouth but already six important checks have been completed.

Chapter four
Developing the dental health check
– the physical checks

Developing the dental health check – the physical checks

The moment has arrived for the physical examination and, because the patient has their mouth open, they are 'all ears'. If you fail to communicate during this part of the appointment – or immediately afterwards – it really is a lost opportunity to demonstrate you care.

7 Health of the teeth

It is useful to let the patient know what the teeth are being checked for. This is not, as dentists will commonly recite, for 'decay, cracks, breaks, wear, abrasions, abfractions', etc., but for health. Remember, patients are hoping for a *clean bill of health*. Comments such as 'Right, let's see how healthy your teeth are', 'All the teeth look healthy' or 'The teeth look healthy, except for...' will fit the bill here.

8 Health and stability of restorations

Although dentists tend to check restorations at the same time as checking teeth, patients think of restorations as separate from the tooth tissue itself. And after all, restorations have entirely different properties. So, when restorations are checked for health and stability, patients should be told these entirely different structures have been checked separately (and hopefully, are stable and healthy).

9 Health of the gums

I've watched and listened to hundreds of dentists measuring pocket depths and recording numbers but only heard a proportion of them discussing the results of the check on gum health with patients. I've also discovered a wide variety of views on what might constitute an 'acceptable' level of gum health.

I often ask dentists if they only discuss gum health and measures to improve it if there are signs of active disease and existing gum damage or if they feel that advice is needed to combat risks of gum inflammation when known causative factors or early warning signs of damage exist. I also ask them how they report the finding of health to those patients who show no signs of gum inflammation or damage at all. The key is that all patients deserve feedback on the health of their gums and what their risks might be for future gum problems. And when they get useful and meaningful feedback, they engage and respond very well. I particularly love practices that use patient-friendly systems for measuring and communicating gum health information (e.g. PreViser), but even in-practice reference protocols or meaningful explanations of the BPE are appreciated. Remember, patients are more responsive to discussions about health than about potential problems.

10 <u>Presence of plaque</u>

I understand the presence of plaque is one indication of risks to gum health. It is also the most accessible risk for patients to identify personally. In short, if it's there, the mouth isn't healthy. Therefore, I recommend the presence of plaque is assessed and discussed separately from the health of the gums as measured by the perio probe (or prodding, as it appears to patients). The presence of plaque can also be linked directly to the first question of the Dental Health Check. Soft plaque deposits can be pointed out to patients as the easiest way to tell if the mouth is indeed healthy or not.

Developing the dental health check – the physical checks

If any patient can find and remove soft plaque with a fingernail, toothbrush, floss or interdental aid, this can be regarded as a sign of a lack of health in the mouth until it is completely removed. By the action of checking for plaque, dentists can help patients focus on what they have to do at home to keep dentally healthy. Most dentists do usually mention plaque or use some other word for the deposits on the teeth and gums or they give a little oral hygiene advice, but they see this check as part of the whole gum health check. Separating plaque out as a check on its own elevates the importance of this entity, and gives increased weight to the importance of controlling it. Referring to hard plaque also helps patients understand why hard deposits form and that these can be prevented if soft plaque is controlled every day.

11 The health of the inside of the mouth – also the oral cancer check

The dental terminology I would most like to encourage dentists to change is how they describe the inside of the mouth. The description 'soft tissues' may be understood between health professionals but, for many patients, the mouth is not what would come to mind first. Ask any middle-aged woman if her dentist checks her soft tissues and the result may be raised eyebrows and a 'That sounds rude!' comment but, sadly, I think a more significant failing is that, when questioned, patients do not know exactly what the soft tissues are. Some say 'The tongue?', 'The cheeks?', 'The gums?' and some 'An oral cancer check?' There is a huge benefit in adopting specific language when doing this check and not just assuming that patients will know what is going on as the tongue is thrust from side to side and to point to door and ceiling.

Action points
Remember to let the patient know that all parts of the mouth are being checked for health – not for problems

Make sure you inform the patient you have carried out an oral cancer check as well as checked areas that can't be seen with the naked or even corrected eye

Dentists could tell patients that when they check the inside of the mouth they are looking at the tongue, lips, cheeks and skin for health. Remember this by using the abbreviation TLCs – many thanks to a practice in Kent for that mnemonic. After the tongue gymnastics routine, it's useful to say to patients: 'The inside of your mouth all looks healthy. Oh, and by the way, that was your oral cancer check.' After all, 63% of patients tell me in my questionnaire that oral cancer screening is very important to them, and it is comforting to have confirmation that an oral cancer screen has been completed. Most patients' shoulders will drop in relaxation if this feedback is well delivered. Now, one or two dentists have indicated to me that they would hate to highlight the fact that they are completing oral cancer screens just in case they have to send patients for further investigation, and they may be worried. Wake up and smell the coffee, friends! These patients worry the minute you suggest another investigation anyway and it's more important to get a speedy diagnosis and either treatment under way or cancer ruled out.

12 The health of hidden areas and the bone
Radiographs are what dentists use to check the health of areas inside, under and between the teeth, and to check the health of the bone levels. Although most dentists only take radiographs every few Dental Health Checks, it is clear to me that most do check the hidden areas and the bone during every Dental Health Check by referring to past radiographs. It would be helpful to tell patients this check is being done each time. So, there we have a 12-point Dental Health Check.

Chapter five
Developing an individual dental health check

I estimate that several hundred dentists now carry out the Dental Health Check and each one has their individual style, including many who have adapted the idea from hearing me talk about the Dental Health Check at meetings, or from colleagues who have found it useful in other practices. Many have developed Dental Health Reports to confirm to patients just how thorough and complete the Dental Health Check is. Some have tick boxes, others smiley faces or boxes to fill in, and more and more are giving red, amber or green (RAG) assessments of health of each aspect checked. I am impressed by those who give their patients the report to take away, having first identified the areas of the mouth that need extra attention or any recommended attention to homecare or lifestyle changes. Having a structure of this kind is impressive to patients who will feel their dentist is rigorously assessing them. I like my clients to evolve their own Dental Health Check.

Some practitioners check additional areas including:
- Current plaque control routines
- How healthy their diet is
- The health of the jaw
- The health and comfort of the bite (occlusion)
- The health of areas outside the mouth, including the lymph glands, muscles, skin and facial symmetry

Others may separate out the checks on the health of the hidden areas and the health of the bone, combine the lifestyle and medical risks checks or use a dental health risk programme such as PreViser, or an in-depth oral cancer screening device such as Veloscope.

Developing an individual dental health check

I think it is useful to communicate the number of aspects covered in the Dental Health Check – it is usually greater than patients imagine and therefore should sound impressive. In order to help all team members understand and communicate the breadth and depth of the regular Dental Health Check, I do feel it is important to sit down with the team to work through the practice's own Dental Health Check and determine the specific number of checks, and the reasons for each, so that the team can discuss the value of the Dental Health Check with patients and answer any questions.

And please don't forget to define:
1 Your New Patient or Initial Dental Health Check will inevitably be bigger than the routine Dental Health Check. This will include items such as dental history, mouth charting and all the checks that will later only be investigated if symptoms present themselves
2 Your Children's – or Young Persons' – Dental Health Check, which will include checks for growth or developmental progress, and home supervisory approach (parental supervision)

I find it useful to tell patients that the DHC has at least two primary purposes:
1 To tell patients how healthy they are in each of the (12) aspects of the Dental Health Check
2 To give patients any advice necessary to improve or maintain dental health

This latter purpose could be a treatment plan detailing options, appointments and costs or it could be referral to a therapist, therapist/hygienist or specialist, or it could be the instruction such as 'Keep using the interdental brushes'.

Action points

Organise a practice meeting to discuss and define the Dental Health Checks in your practice: the new patient DHC, the regular DHC and the children's DHC

Always give a specific take-home message to your patients – such as what you would like them to continue doing or start doing; or when you would like to see them next or why and when they next need to see a therapist/ hygienist

I maintain that there is always valuable professional advice to be given and the vague 'You're fine' is inadequate and lazy. I think what it really means is 'There's nothing here for *me* to do'. Yet, if a very healthy patient is to remain healthy, surely the health professional should be giving specific advice such as 'Make sure you continue to remove plaque from between these teeth as often as you can – preferably every day', or 'Just be careful when you do go to university not to increase the frequency of your sugar intake and beware of fizzy drinks and constant grazing when you're studying'.

Always find something specific to say to very healthy patients, including the reasons why they should continue to see the therapist/ hygienist, even if only once every one or two years, or what they should continue to be doing at home. I believe the generalisations 'Keep up the good work' or 'Keep doing what you're doing' are dangerous to say to patients.

Remember, in the absence of information, we all fill in the gaps with what we believe is right and, if you just tell a patient it's okay to do what they've been doing lately – and they've been skipping the occasional day in terms of interdental cleaning – you may have just given them permission to skip more!

Chapter six
Making sure the dental health check happens

I've always been aware that what I ask dentists to do is difficult. They have developed their examination and communications habits over years, decades even, and then overnight they are expected to change to a whole new positive, health-focused approach. The physical amount of change involved in moving from most exams or check-ups to Dental Health Checks is not particularly huge – generally, I ask dentists to introduce two or, perhaps, three additional questions into their existing routines – but I do ask them to take many of their previous checks 'out of the closet' to be more obvious to patients, and to communicate that each check has been completed and, ideally, that the result is one of positive health. This quality of change is very hard indeed and, even with the best intentions, old habits are hard to break. So, implementing the change to delivering the Dental Health Check must be a team game and I believe that dental nurses play a pivotal role in ensuring change happens. Ideally, the Dental Heath Check becomes a protocol or a framework, which means a form should be filled in or a checklist of all essential aspects run through. The only person who can fill in that checklist in the surgery is the dental nurse. To start the process of changing to the full Dental Health Check appointment, I ask dentists to remember to ask the first, orienting, scene-setting question, 'How healthy do you feel your teeth and gums are?' and then proceed through their checks pretty much as normal – remembering, where possible, to give a short report on the health of each aspect checked.

Making sure the dental health check happens

Meanwhile, as well as recording the essential data as usual, nurses tick off all aspects they know have been completed and, preferably, mentioned to patients. At the end of the Dental Health Check, the dentist can ask the nurse if he/she has 'got all the details'. If any of the check areas have not been obviously assessed or made obvious to patients, the nurse simply prompts the dentist to continue with the assessment by asking 'Can you tell me about (the patient's) restorations?' or 'How does (the patient) feel about the appearance of her teeth and gums?' If necessary, the routine is explained as a new one to make sure all areas are recorded. Eventually, the nurse helps the dentist to communicate the fact that all points on the checklist have been completed. If the practice is really going to prove to patients that the Dental Health Check is broader and deeper than they originally believed, it would seem useful to give patients a written report of their state of health. Such a document should be very simple, reducing the potential for conflicting reports between practitioners in a practice, but also meaningful and valuable to patients. It strikes me that there is a similarity between taking a car for a service and the patient bringing their mouth in for a full Dental Health Check. In both cases, the customer or patient has no idea if or how specific checks are completed, but it is reassuring nonetheless to receive the list of ticks against any number of motor parts and functions afterwards. There is a palpable feeling of relief that breakdown is less imminent and that there is a value to the service fee.

So, my advice is first of all to note that each check has been completed. Secondly, a very simple 'healthy' or 'not healthy' would seem to be adequate in terms of reassurance, although at least one more option works well, for instance: a 'healthy for now' or a 'must do something now' type of advice. Or even 'red', 'amber' or 'green' status. Many of the practices with whom I have worked in the past 10 years have now developed some form of Dental Health Report to be given to patients at the end of the Dental Health Check. I have supplied these practices with my first basic format for such a report, and some samples from previous clients. It never fails to impress me how each practice then individualises the reports to suit their own Dental Health Checks and practice style. I am also very grateful to the team at Henry Schein who developed a Dental Health Check report custom screen for EXACT, which many of my clients using Software of Excellence's program have adapted and now complete on-screen for printing out for the patient at reception or in a treatment co-ordinator's room. I prefer a printed card or sheet to be given to patients, particularly if the practice is hoping to build and expand, as I believe that a few printed report cards are more likely to be discussed with friends and colleagues. But there is always a requirement to keep a record or copy in the patient notes. Computer-generated reports are easier to keep for records purposes and, if these are used, I suggest the report is folded inside-out before being given to patients – just a little tip to avoid the potential for the report being lost in piles of paperwork at home.

Making sure the dental health check happens

Patient responses

Practices that introduce the Dental Health Check and Report do find that the health focus gives new energy and importance to the regular appointments and involves nurses in the feedback provided more than ever before. There appears to be an enhanced appreciation from patients who achieve excellent health. I would estimate that 80% of patients value the card/report. If the occasional patient fails to value the report, this is their own view, but I believe that impressing the majority of patients outweighs an occasional neutral or negative response. In mixed practices, the Dental Health Check and Report provide a point of differentiation from the usual check-up appointments provided under the NHS, although, at the time of writing, we have yet to see how the NHS Oral Health Assessment becomes part of mainstream NHS care and how it might differ from the Dental Health Check provided privately. As a further benefit, team members are more confident in the value of the appointments and the whole service.

The Dental Health Check and Report – promotional opportunities

Once the Dental Health Check has been defined, there are numerous ways in which this appointment can be described to define value in the practice.

New patients

At last, private practices have something tangible to offer patients, and more than 'check-ups and X-rays' for higher fees than patients remember from their check-ups of the past! As long as receptionists have been part of the team working to define the practice's Dental Health Check – or have been steeped in knowledge and understanding of this most important appointment – we can expect receptionists to positively respond to two of three of the most common initial requests made by new patients.

Patient:
'Are you taking on new patients?' or 'Do you do NHS?'
Receptionist:
'We're a fully private practice. Would you like me to tell you how we would look after you?'
Patient:
'Yes.'
Receptionist:
'Your first appointment would be for an initial 14-point Dental Health Check, and that would cost £x. During that appointment, the dentist will find out how you feel about your mouth and check 14 aspects of your dental health. You'd then get a report of how healthy you are in each of the 14 areas and advice on anything that would need to be done to get you or keep you dentally healthy. Is this the sort of thing you're looking for?'

Who could say no?

Making sure the dental health check happens

Action points

- Involve your whole team in defining protocols for the Dental Health Check
- Ensure your nurse is your DHC champion
- Consider the introduction of a written report card for patients to take away – appropriately branded, it reinforces your role in the care of the patient's dental health

In-practice promotion

The Dental Health Check and Report are fantastic opportunities to show patients just how much care the practice takes over their dental health. Many practices have found it useful to produce posters or leaflets to explain all of the checks provided. Newsletter and website articles can also back up the value provided. Of course, the best promotional aid of all is the Dental Health Report and it is common for receptionists to offer to send/email copies of a blank report to potential new patients to show them what is covered in the essential first appointment.

External promotion

Promoting the x-point Dental Health Check externally can give a very positive impression of the care provided by the practice.

Standard literature

One of the most challenging implications of introducing the Dental Health Check and Report for many practices has been the need to update standard letters, forms and literature making sure the old 'check-up' term is replaced with 'Dental Health Check' (and hopefully a few words of explanation) on reminders, follow-up letters, estimates, invoices, leaflets, post-treatment factsheets, signage, etc. I always recommend appointing a language champion from the team to make sure all communications reflect the new order whenever the Dental Health Check is introduced.

Chapter seven
Building hygiene

Building hygiene

If the Dental Health Check is the most important appointment patients attend, then the hygiene appointment is also high up there. In the successful health-focused practice, at least 90% of patients will visit the therapist/hygienist at least once per year and, many of these, twice per year or more. If practices do not have a therapist/hygienist, then the dentist (frustrated therapist/hygienist) will provide the hygiene appointment and I believe it is essential in this sort of practice that the hygiene appointment is well defined, explained and promoted to patients. Over the years, my practices' patients have reported that providing care, advice and treatments to ensure the health of teeth and gums is the most important clinical requirement, and the second most important aspect of the practice overall. In 2010/11 this was very important to 82% of patients. In contrast, the skills of the therapist/hygienist were rated as 'very important' to only 57% of patients, although admittedly this statistic has been rising steadily over the past 10 years.

Why the difference?

Therapist/hygienists tell me their whole professional life is dedicated to helping patients achieve higher levels of dental health and that this is the focus of each and every appointment. The entire dental team agrees with this but, for some reason, patients fail to appreciate the importance of the therapist/hygienist and the hygiene appointment. In fact, it is very common for patients of excellent preventive practices with therapist/hygienists in situ to rate the skills and attitudes of therapist/hygienists very highly – yet the 'importance' ratings are still disappointing. Surely if patients knew what the team knows, the importance ratings should be similar?

I blame dentists for failing to adequately explain the purpose of the hygiene appointment, what to expect during a hygiene appointment, why it is important to keep to programmes of hygiene appointments and what patients can expect as a result. I believe these failures may be due to laziness on the part of dentists; perhaps a lack of interest in terms of what gets done by someone else; an abdication of patient motivation to therapist/hygienists or a lack of focus on the importance of health to patients themselves. Dentists may have been well-meaning. The dentist who knows exactly what therapist/hygienists can do for patients knows that each patient's regular attendance to a therapist/hygienist will make all the difference. And if he or she recommends a hygiene visit, the patient should comply. Yes?

This may have been the case in years gone by, when dentists were revered for their white tunics and professional advice, but today's patients need to understand why they are given advice and decide for themselves whether to comply or not. From my experience, patients are more likely to cancel or fail to turn up for a hygiene appointment than a dentist appointment. They may appear to comply with the dentist's advice to see a therapist/hygienist whilst in the surgery but their attitude can be deduced from failure to keep to regular hygiene appointment schedules. A quick calculation will give you an indication of the loss rate in your practice.

Building hygiene

Let's look at a practice with 1,000 adult patients attending regularly. Let's say, on average, 90% of these patients will benefit from two hygiene appointments per year. This equates to 900 hours – or 19.5 hours per week worked. That's nearly three days per week for every 1,000 patients, not including time required for serious periodontal treatments, family or children's appointments and treatment appointments if your therapist/hygienist is also a therapist. My own expectation of my clients is that for every five days of general practice dentistry, I would expect at least four days fully booked hygiene appointments to be required.

Not all practices achieve this ratio without some serious attention – although my star clients beat it hands down and have more hygiene time booked than dentist time. No wonder therapist/hygienists have sought direct access so they can control the flow of information and advice to patients. They want to ensure patients see the value in programmes of hygiene visits and hygiene advice and to bypass the controlling health professional who does not give 'best professional encouragement' to attend. I recommend redefining the hygiene appointment with a more beady eye on communicating the need to improve health, and then looking at the language of the referral from the dentist. What is a hygiene appointment? What happens in the ideal hygiene appointment?

Action points

Elevate the importance of the hygiene appointment so it is more highly valued by patients

Change the language you use for a hygiene referral – banning the words 'scale and polish'

<u>In most of my practices, therapist/hygienists do three main things</u>:

1. They assess or re-assess gum health and home care routines.
2. They remove hard plaque.
3. They work with patients on the things they can do (the skills, tools and techniques they can use) to control damaging dental plaque (removing it from every surface of every tooth, every day) so that patients can become more dentally healthy.

Therapist/hygienists tell me the most important of these three things is the work they do with patients on the skills they need for their home care regime – not the plaque removal bit! So, why, oh why, is the appointment known as a 'scale and polish' or 'scaling/cleaning' – the least useful part of the appointment if we are focused on improving health – in 90% of practices across the land? When dentists refer patients for a 'scale and polish', the patient expects something to be done to them – i.e. the therapist/hygienist is responsible for improving their dental health, not the patient. The therapist/hygienist knows that patients expect something to be done to them, so feel obliged to spend the greater part of the appointment time removing hard plaque, leaving a few minutes to rattle off a few homecare instructions. Now, I'm led to believe that the removal of hard plaque does not affect dental health long-term unless daily plaque removal habits also change. So, the focus and language of the hygiene appointment has to change in order to deliver what therapist/hygienists are aiming for and what patients want. The reasons for a referral to the therapist/hygienist have to become much more specific and meaningful to patients.

Chapter eight
The hygiene protocol

Just as the Dental Health Check must be clearly defined, so too must the maintenance hygiene appointment. And it is therapist/hygienists who must lead this process. I believe all practices should have a clear protocol in place for each type of hygiene appointment. Such a protocol is particularly useful to remind dentists and team members exactly what goes on in each hygiene appointment so they can refer intelligently and accurately support the patient to attend.
Where there are multiple therapist/hygienists in practices, the protocol ensures that patients can expect a similar experience no matter which therapist/hygienist they see. And the protocol also reminds practice owners to recruit and select for therapist/hygienists who deliver the most useful and meaningful care and advice.

Protocol for Maintenance Hygiene Appointment
Greet
1. *Introduce self*
2. *Do you know/what do you know about why you've come for a hygiene appointment?*
   (Explain importance of health of gums; how health controlled; role of therapist/hygienist if necessary)

Refer to notes
3. *Check and refer to notes from dentist/medical details and risks. Notes/comments from last appointment*

Three questions
4. *How healthy do you feel your mouth is just now? (Mirrors dentist's focusing question)*
5. *What's your routine for looking after your mouth and removing plaque?*
6. *Do you know why it's important to remove plaque?*

The hygiene protocol

Share
7 *Examine mouth*
8 *Explain where soft plaque collecting and (maybe) causing inflammation/hard plaque or making control difficult*
9 *Inform why that's a problem and possible consequences*

Remove plaque
10 *Remove as much as possible – bring back if needed**
11 *Discuss plaque control*
12 *Discuss skills, tools and techniques to remove damaging plaque from every surface of every tooth*
13 *Including why it's important to remove plaque every day*

Discuss habits
14 *When could you find two minutes twice a day?*
15 *Can you try this bit – let me check that you can get into this area (or similar)*

Reinforcement
16 *Remember you can buy (specific tools) at reception. These cost...*
17 *Reinforcement of main points of advice – including written information*
18 *Recommendation for future visits/changes to programme of hygiene visits for future health*

* Additional protocols needed on ideal programmes of appointments to review home care and progress and complete hard plaque removal

The language of hygiene

As I said, in my clients' practices, words such as 'scale and polish', 'scaling' or even 'cleaning' are banned. These are all words with definite dental meanings but only describe a small part of what happens in a health-focused hygiene appointment. 'Toothbrushing' is also a banned term in most situations because the patient is likely to have a narrow understanding of what is meant by this. When a dentist or a therapist/hygienist talks about 'cleaning', he or she usually means 'removal of all the plaque from every surface of every tooth every day'. A patient may think 'cleaning' means borrowing his or her spouse's toothbrush, scrubbing it around the outside of their teeth once per day to remove stains and little bits of food. This is what they have been doing for years and they are not about to change the habits of a lifetime without good reason. So, it's time to ditch the bad language and redefine the hygiene appointment and hygiene referral in a way that the patient will begin to understand what visits are all about. In order to help patients understand why they are being referred to the practice therapist/hygienist and why the appointments are necessary, dentists again have to be very specific in their language. They also have to explain the importance of the visits. Although it takes much longer to explain this than just sending patients for the old 'scale and polish', the practice is always rewarded with more patient compliance. *Plaque Story III* is the title I have given to a series of three-part explanations that have been shown to be highly effective in changing the way patients think about their hygiene visits and their attendance behaviour. In practices where it is used effectively, patient appreciation of the importance of the skills of the therapist/hygienist is always increased in future patient surveys.

The hygiene protocol

1. Sheila, you have plaque (here and here/too much of it/etc.)
2. The problem with plaque is that it causes gum inflammation (which then causes problems to mouth health, tooth health/could cause tooth loss/we now believe that if inflammation is controlled, this may help protect the heart and other parts of the whole body from future damage – whatever the team is comfortable explaining)
3. So I'm going to recommend an initial one/two hygiene visits (or a programme of hygiene visits) for you. During these visits our therapist/hygienist will:
a) Assess or re-assess your gum health and your home care habits
b) Remove this hard plaque that is building up on your teeth and under your gums
c) But, most importantly, she will work with you on
  - Skills
  - Tools
  - Techniques or habits to help you remove the soft plaque
1. From every surface
2. Of every tooth
3. Every day

<u>If you can do this effectively, you will</u>
1. Keep your mouth healthier
2. Reduce your risk of future tooth/gum problems and treatments
3. And you may be keeping your whole body healthier too

This story should be told every time a patient is referred to the practice therapist/hygienist and every time existing patients are encouraged to keep up their hygiene visits.

Also...
1 After this initial visit/these initial visits
2 We will see if your daily plaque control has improved
3 And we will re-assess your risk of mouth damage

And...
How well you respond to the therapist/hygienist's advice will
1 Determine how often you will need to see her
2 What sort of regime you will need to follow at home in order to keep healthy
3 Determine the programme or dental health plan we will suggest to help keep you healthy long-term (see below)

Hygiene programmes for long-term health
One of the results of patients' failure to appreciate the importance of the therapist/hygienists' skills and also one of the big frustrations of excellent therapist/hygienists is the patients' failure to keep to recommended recall intervals for their visits. Patients need to be encouraged to attend regularly. I like to hear dentists and their teams routinely defining an ideal programme of hygiene visits for each patient and routinely using the words 'hygiene programme'. This makes it clear that hygiene visits are a habit patients should get into – they are not one-off treatment appointments. If the practice truly believes that hygiene appointments are helpful in maintaining health, I like clinicians to give permission to the whole team to use the illustrated sound bites.

The hygiene protocol

Action points

Redefine the hygiene appointment and introduce language which will help patients understand its value

Constantly encourage patients to attend their hygiene visits regularly

Hygiene appointment sound bites

For many patients, it is more important to see our therapist/hygienist regularly than it is to see our dentist regularly. Our therapist/hygienist helps to keep you healthy – dentists mainly repair damage that happens when you let health slip. Are you sure you can't fit that appointment in soon?

Our dentists believe that 90% of the treatment they provide is totally and utterly preventable*. Our therapist/hygienists help you to prevent the need for treatments. Can I encourage you to keep that appointment, or re-book it soon?

Our therapist/hygienists work with patients on the skills, tools and techniques they need to keep dentally healthy long-term. For most patients this is more important than the scaling and polishing, and if you can follow their advice, future hygiene appointments should be much less uncomfortable.

(*attrib. Ken James, circa 1992)

Chapter nine
Dental plans

Dental plans

I have always been a fan of plans in dental practices and although patients can prefer capitation plans to maintenance plans, I have found that maintenance is a much fairer and safer option for both patients and practices. Maintenance plans are easier to price accurately and for the patient there is a direct correlation between what they get and what they are paying for. However, many practices are failing to communicate to patients the biggest difference a plan can make – namely, that it is likely to be better for their dental health. I know this because I regularly encourage my client practices to audit the difference between plan patients, private patients and NHS patients in terms of treatment prescribed and attendance patterns. In all but two or three practices so far, the results have revealed a surprising disparity between NHS, pay-as-you-go patients and plan patients. On the whole, plan patients definitely keep to tighter recall intervals – keeping to Dental Health Check and hygiene visits pretty much on the recall timescales that are prescribed for them. But even with the best will in the world, NHS and fully private pay-as-you-go patients tend to let their dental and hygiene appointments drift. The first practice that completed this audit for me – in the days when almost all patients were recommended to return for their six-monthly appointment – we were shocked to discover that while plan patients were actually returning for their Dental Health Check every six to eight months, private patients – who were believed to be just as 'regular' – were returning every 14 to 17 months. These patients were often surprised when they were told how long it had been since their last appointment!

Even more shocking was the size of the difference in the value of treatments prescribed (corrected for differences in patients' fiscal status) when patients were eventually seen. It makes sense to expect that patients who have not been seen for longer may need more treatment than those seen regularly, but an average increased value of treatment plans for these less frequently attending private patients was 69% by value. In other words, private patients needed 69% more treatment (by value) than plan patients when they saw the dentist. With audited statistics like these, the practice could prove that the maintenance plan option was not just better value for money for patients compared to paying for comparable appointments, but much more likely to result in a healthier mouth and less treatment. Most importantly, this practice could then recommend plan membership for good ethical reasons. Other practices have reported similar differences in terms of Dental Health Check and hygiene appointment attendance and differences in the value of treatments prescribed up to 100% more for the less frequently attending private patients. Furthermore, some practices have found that the differences in attendance intervals and prescribed treatments for NHS patients can be even greater. It will be interesting to find out whether prescribed treatments will increase or decrease following the implementation of NICE guidelines on exam intervals. My own belief is that whatever appointment intervals are recommended and explained to patients, compliance will generally be better among patients who are in a programme to which they have committed via direct debit payments.

Dental plans

Action points

Audit the difference in attendance patterns between pay-as-you-go and plan patients, and tell patients if there is any difference in results

Encourage patients onto your dental plan because this is the best way you can organise to keep patients healthy

The differences in patient behaviour have long been known by the insurance industry, local government, opticians, publishers – indeed, any organisation that depends on regular purchases. These organisations know the public is much more likely to keep up regular purchases/less likely to default, and more likely to continue to feel a loyalty to a brand, if a direct debit or a standing order can be secured. Customers also take longer to change purchasing behaviour if a direct debit or standing order is in place.

In dental care, we know most patients who pay by monthly direct debit are more likely to keep up their regular visits to the practice, pretty much on time. The customer will make sure he gets his money's worth after arranging for regular payments and the patient will make sure he visits at the recommended interval. So, the way patients pay for their dental care does affect their behaviour. Their visiting behaviour, in turn, affects their dental health. I plead with practices to stop telling patients they should join the plan because it is better value on the face value of the appointments covered or because it's easier to pay for care or for the included insurances. Instead, I recommend patients are urged to join plans because this is the best way to keep them healthy.

Chapter ten
One more thing – sterilisation and patient protection

One more thing – sterilisation and patient protection

Most clinicians and teams tell me patients don't understand and fail to appreciate the considerable care, attention and expenditure that have gone into keeping them safe in the practice. They tell me patients never ask about sterilisation. Yet, in my questionnaires, 'sterilisation/patient protection' has been consistently very important to patients since the early 1990s – this aspect of practice shot to the top of the list of patients' ratings of importance just after the first Panorama programme about David Acer – the Florida dentist who was accused of passing on HIV infection to six patients (he was never convicted). Since then, every time a local or national story has broken about sterilisation failures, this becomes the patients' number one priority for a while, and then it drops back to third or fourth place on the listing. Of course, patients care deeply about their practices' attention to sterilisation and safety. They know, absolutely, that if they were to be taken into their local hospital this weekend, they might end up with MRSA or *C. diff*. If they had a meal out, the danger is salmonella, and sitting in a grubby Jacuzzi – Legionnaires' disease. They also know, absolutely, and without knowledge of the real risks and incidences, that there is a potential risk of getting HIV from their dentist. So they are watching you. They are watching how everyone handles instruments and disinfects surfaces. They believe that when instruments are dropped on the floor, they are picked up, wiped and put back in drawers – after all, we've all believed in the five-second rule at home once or twice, where it doesn't count if a dropped biscuit is picked up within five seconds!

They believe that the mouthwash, filled up to within two inches of the top of the beaker, was used by the previous patient, and they surreptitiously check it for lipstick marks before gulping when requested. They believe that grubby marks or dust on the skirting boards in the loo are symptoms of a practice that doesn't care enough about cleanliness – or sterilisation. They are also checking what the team members touch – especially when they are wearing gloves, which highlight the potential of danger. Observing a dentist picking up a pen or pushing a switch with a gloved finger merely illustrates how he or she might be protecting themselves (from any germs on the switch) rather than protecting the patient who is next touched with the side of the glove that touched the switch. Patients make assumptions about sterilisation behaviour and, particularly as sterilisation has become increasingly moved to discrete areas out of the patients' sight, it becomes ever more important to prove the practice's attention to this area. But – unlike providing proof for CQC, RQIA, HIS or HIW – this does not involve arduous paper trails and bulging files. Instead, a little attention to behaviour and the 'theatre of practice' is required. This can be a great and fun topic for a practice meeting. In how many ways can the team demonstrate to patients their attention to sterilisation? The record so far is 33 new ways, but I would settle for five or six key action points that can be agreed and implemented among the team to help patients understand your attention to sterilisation measures.

One more thing – sterilisation and patient protection

<u>Impressing patients regarding attention to sterilisation</u>

1. *Invest in great signage for your decontamination room. Glass walls with* **Sterilisation Area** *really do impress – but simple signs do the job, too.*
2. *If your decontamination room is tucked away out of sight, invest in* **To the Sterilisation Area** *signs – your team may know where it is, but patients need to be confident that you have one.*
3. *Make sure team members talk about taking trays or boxes to the sterilisation room – no more silently slipping in and out of the surgery (within reason!) – make what you do between every patient obvious.*
4. *Talk about sterilising or sterilised instruments in the surgeries ('I'll take these to the steriliser' or 'Can I have a sterile pointy thing?' highlight that your actions are routine.)*
5. *Make sure mouthwash is only set out for patients when needed, or at least after they enter the surgery. It may seem efficient to have it ready, but this does look like the last patient used the beaker! And rows of beakers lined up at the ready are banned!*
6. *Role-play conversations for when instruments are dropped. It may seem wasteful to say 'I'll put that through the steriliser', but the patient might believe it will be picked up and used on them if you don't make your intentions obvious.*
7. *Enforce strict glove behaviour protocols. No touching anything non-sterile with gloved hands.*
8. *Take down your 'dirty' signs and labels on boxes. Surely the words should be 'sterilised' and 'not sterilised'?*
9. *Insist on absolute cleanliness. In general, two hours every day for general cleaning keeps a two-surgery practice spotless.*

Action points
Engage the team in coming up with five or six key ways to make sterilisation routines obvious to patients

10 *Keep surgery surfaces clutter free. A tidy surface is more likely to have been re-sterilised in the patients' eyes.*

11 *Mention that you are disinfecting your hands/gloves when you are doing this. Help patients to notice your routines.*

12 *Finally, consider giving your cross-infection routines a name of their very own – Re-sterilising or Decontamination is not something that is tagged onto the end of every appointment, but an activity in its own right. Do this, and your receptionist can say 'Mrs Dentist will be with you shortly, Mrs Patient, just give her and Lorna a few minutes for re-sterilising and they'll be right with you.'*

Chapter eleven
Conclusion

As this book was being written, a number of things were happening in – and to – UK dentistry. The profession was preparing for yet another new dental contract in England and further changes to the provision of NHS dentistry; the legal framework was becoming scarier, with more dentists finding themselves at the wrong end of a GDC investigation or civil litigation; patients were becoming even choosier and more in need of good reasons to spend their money in private practices; and more practices were chasing a seemingly static pond of new patients.

Many practices were gearing up to meet an increasingly consumerist society with great branding, promotion and social media strategies. In short, the environment was and still is becoming even more competitive.

My own consultancy is changing from one where I am helping already successful practices become more so to one where the 'rescue' project is not uncommon. Almost all practices are seeking more patients and more profits. I have always said to my practices: 'You only get the patients you deserve.'

In many cases, I believe the rescue project becomes necessary because practices stand still, fail to adapt to more demanding patients, ignoring the need to seek change, improvement and excellence, and fail to let patients know exactly what they do for them.

Conclusion

I firmly believe that no amount of sexy new technology for perfecting the clinical work and no degree of technical skill and artistry will bring success to a practice unless the approach to dental health is explained and promoted to patients on an individual basis. I hope this book helps you demonstrate – with pride – just how much you care.